THE
POWER
OF
POSITIVE
PRAYING

THE POWER OF POSITIVE PRAYING

PROVOCATIVE HINTS FOR PEACE
AND POWER THROUGH CONFIDENT
PRAYER

JOHN BISAGNO

ZondervanPublishingHouse
Grand Rapids, Michigan

A Division of HarperCollinsPublishers

THE POWER OF POSITIVE PRAYING
Copyright © 1965 by Zondervan Publishing House
Grand Rapids, Michigan

Requests for information should be addressed to:
Zondervan Publishing House
Grand Rapids, Michigan 49530

First Zondervan Publishing House edition 1972

ISBN 0-310-21212-X

Printed in the United States of America

95   96 / LP / 55   54   53

CONTENTS

PREFACE

Since 1952 I have traveled throughout much of America serving the Lord in the abundant field of evangelism. I have come to believe that, beyond a doubt, the greatest need of religious America is prayer. From every quarter the cry arises for more faithfulness and consistency from God's people, yet little comes forth. Why do we grow so little? Why do we win so few? Why are we weak and powerless? Because we pray so little.

Why do our people stay away from prayer meetings in mass? Because most of them know so little of prayer that they are really embarrassed to try. To them, to the Christian lay men and women everywhere, this book is written. Most of us pray little because we do not know what to say to God, or how to say it. This book is written in everyday language for the man in the pew. It is simple. It is practical. You can read it and try it, and find that it works.

If it is helpful to you I shall be grateful to God, who inspired it to my own heart through many faithful ones along the way.

To Linda, March 2011
With much love and
gratefulness for you

Pastor + Sue
I John 2:17

THE
POWER
OF
POSITIVE
PRAYING

CHAPTER 1

ANSWERED PRAYER

Honestly now, wouldn't you be surprised if all your prayers were answered? Have you prayed, or at least thought you were praying, for such a long time for certain things that if they ever happened you would be utterly dumfounded? Did you ever have the experience of sharing with friends some matter about which you were praying? Then your prayer was answered, and you rushed to tell them, "Guess what? My husband really was converted!" (or "We did reach our Sunday school goal," or "Mrs. Jones actually was healed"). Only to have them answer, "Well, what's so strange about that? You were praying for it weren't you?" And you had to admit, "Yes, I guess I was!"

Do you really expect an answer to your prayers? Have not most of us had the sad experience of praying so generally, for so long, that when scattered drops of answered prayer do fall, they are so rare as hardly to be noticed?

Why? Because only about 10 per cent of our prayers are specific, faith-centered petitions. The overwhelming majority of our prayers are far too general to bring a specific answer, or even a slightly recognizable answer amid the general blessings that are going to fall anyway.

We call out, "God bless America, God bless our church, our revival, the missionaries and Christian workers around the world," but seldom have our lives been strengthened by knowing that our prayers for specific events and people have been answered. In fact, we do not know whether our prayers were ever answered!

Away with such empty prayer. Nothing has affected my life or will yours, as learning of this mighty treasure in the storehouse of God's dealings with man. *Answered prayer is not a miracle, it is a law.* It should always be. It may always be. It *will* always be, when the laws are kept and certain rules are observed. It is always to be expected!

Early in my ministry I was greatly affected by the relationship of this fact to the law of revival as preached by Charles G. Finney. His contemporaries said of Mr. Finney that "he prayed down revival." Of which the mighty preacher said simply, "Nonsense. It is neither Scriptural nor logical. Revival is not a reward sent in answer to my much praying. When I pray I do not pray for revival, I pray for myself. I do not beg my Heavenly Father for blessings as though He were deaf, I merely make my requests known and then turn quickly the searchlight of prayer upon my own self. Prayer doesn't change God, it changes you, so that it is consistent for God to do what He wants to do anyway."

When the child of God prays and his prayers are answered, three things have happened: he has prayed in faith believing, he has prayed specifically and has thereby met the conditions of a loving Heavenly Father, and the Father has responded.

Learn these things well. They are basic to the mastery of answered prayer. Answers by a loving Father to a faithful child are not promises held out as rewards, not miraculous, not strange or abnormal, they are the norm. This is as it should be. Meet the conditions—pray and expect—and prayer will be answered.

Were you to turn the temperature down to 32 degrees, and ice formed from water, would you be surprised? No, because a law has been in operation. The physicist does not say, "Let me make you a proposition. If you lower the temperature to 32 degrees, I promise that as a reward, I'll give you ice." He says that there will be ice. It is not a bargain or a deal, not a proposition or a promise. It is not even a reward for having cooled the air. It is a law. Just so, much of what we call Bible promises are actually not promises at all, they are laws, immutable, unchanging laws. God's laws are as unbreakable and steadfast as God Himself. A man may think he breaks a law of God, but, alas, he does not; he only breaks himself upon that law. God's laws cannot be broken.

Examine carefully again, the famed Old Testament verse, II Chronicles 7:14: "If my people, which are called by my name, shall humble themselves, and pray, and seek my face, and turn from their wicked ways; then will I hear from heaven, and will forgive their sin, and will heal their land."

Does this sound like a promise, a bargain, or a law? Observe the wording carefully. It is not as though He says that when these conditions are met I will do thus and so as a reward, but rather, "Then will I hear." Do you not see? Something big is going to happen! It must happen. God's people have fulfilled the conditions, and the results never vary.

We thrill at stories of great saints who have

prayed unwaveringly for twenty, thirty—even fifty years—for specific things as though they held onto God by the skin of their spiritual teeth, thereby proving their great faith. But wait. Must this be the logical conclusion, or might there be the slight possibility that the admonition of James 4:3 could be applicable ("Ye ask and receive not because ye ask amiss")?

Must long, laborious, unanswered prayer always be a sign of great spirituality or could it be an indication that we might be praying erroneously, or that at least there could be a better way to pray?

As we journey through these next pages, perhaps God will have something a bit new for us. Let us be ready, if necessary, to rethink our concept of prayer.

Answered prayer is not abnormal, it is normal. It is not unusual; it is, or can be, your everyday experience—not to be marveled at, but to be expected.

CHAPTER 2

THE PRAYER OF FAITH

How may you be assured of the constant relationship with God that produces answered prayer?

Note carefully that it is a possibility—even a reality. The Scripture says:

> If ye have faith as a grain of mustard seed, ye shall say unto this mountain, Remove hence to yonder place; and it shall remove; and nothing shall be impossible unto you (Matthew 17:20).
>
> All things, whatsoever ye shall ask in prayer, believing, ye shall receive (Matthew 21:22).
>
> All things are possible to him that believeth (Mark 9:23).
>
> Therefore I say unto you, All things whatsoever ye pray and ask for, believe that ye receive them, and ye shall have them (Mark 11:24 A.S.V.).

The secret then, the heart of answered prayer, lies within the key to each of these verses. Believe, believe, believe, believe. You must simply believe that God is *going to* answer your prayer. It must be a prayer of faith. To believe that He can answer, that He is *able*, that He does possess the power to do it, is not faith. It is to believe unhesitatingly that He *will*, that He is on the verge of doing it, and that even now, the answer is on the way.

13

The dictionary defines faith as trust in the honesty and truth of another. The prayer of faith is simply that, trusting, believing that God is honest and will therefore do what He says He will.

Were I to say to you, "Do you believe God can stop communism, revive the U.S.A., or win every unconverted man in your community tonight?" You would most certainly say, "Yes, I know He can, He is surely able!"

But this is not faith. We *think* that it is but it is not!

Let me ask you, not "Do you believe God *can?*" but "Do you believe God *will* do these things?" Would you not have to reply, "Well I'm not sure that He will"?

Remember this: *Faith is not believing God* can. *Faith is believing God will.*

The reason so little is accomplished by most of us is that we expect so little. Most people aim at absolutely nothing in life and hit it right on the head! We pray the same way. We believe that He *can*, but we do not believe that He *will*.

Many times I have driven to a church to preach a series of evangelistic services, my heart filled with great expectancy, only to receive the usual greeting by the pastor and people, "Now don't expect much, we don't." And they were not disappointed.

The story is told of a father who saw his boy returning from the family fishing hole with only one little fish at the bottom of the stringer. "Well, Son," he said, "didn't you catch anything today?"

"No," replied the boy, "Not as many as I'd hoped to, but then I didn't really think I would anyway."

How often have you inquired of a friend of God's blessing upon special services only to hear the reply,

"We didn't have much, but then we didn't really expect to."

Some of the many misconceptions regarding faith should be noted. First, faith is not desire. God does not say, "According to how much you want it, so be it," rather "According to your *faith be it unto you*" (Matthew 9:29).

Many people have a "Hollywood religion" attitude toward faith. A famed star will give a movie magazine testimonial about an opening night and relate that his great faith saw him through to success, because he just knew if he wanted it to be a success badly enough, it was bound to be one. But longing, wanting, desiring are not faith. Desire, rightly directed, can produce faith, and may lead you to faith, but in itself is not faith.

Faith is not goodness. It is not according to our deserts, not how much we feel we deserve something, but according to how much we believe God will give it to us. To be sure, you will want to be free from known sin and be right with God in your heart. But even this righteousness is not a substitute for faith.

Have you not often experienced a genuine re-dedication of your heart and, for a time at least, entered into a state of real rightness with God, only to be disappointed to find that your prayers still went unanswered?

When the powerless disciples asked Jesus why they could not heal the lunatic boy, the Master said it was because of their faithlessness, and reprimanded the whole generation, calling them faithless and perverse. Sin—perversity—was part of it, but faithlessness was an equal part.

It is not faith in *faith* that the Master rewards but faith in God!

Don't get the idea that if you can only muster more faith, you will be effective in prayer. Faith is not some mysterious commodity to be sought after. You do not need more faith; you need to learn to appropriate the faith you already have. Ours is not a problem of the amount of faith, but of the direction of faith. It is not faith in faith, but faith in God. Do not err by thinking, "Ah, but I have no faith," for you have.

Faith is a cheap commodity. Everyone has faith. Atheists have faith—faith that there is no God, no hereafter. Animals possess faith. They display the utmost of faith in their masters, as do children in their parents.

Faith is the heart of history. You never saw George Washington or Thomas Jefferson, and yet you believe that they lived.

Faith is the heart of life. You go to a doctor whose name you cannot pronounce. He gives you a prescription you cannot read. You take it to a pharmacist you have never seen. He gives you medicine you do not understand and yet you take it. All in trusting, sincere *faith!*

Best of all, the faith of Jesus Christ is potentially yours. Examine again the words of Paul. "The life which I now live in the flesh I live by the faith *of* the son of God" (Galatians 2:20). Note that he does not say "I live this life by faith *in* the son of God," but rather, "*by the* faith *of* the son of God."

What does it mean? Simply this: When I became a Christian—trusted Him and received Him as my Saviour—a spiritual union took place between me and the Son of God. At that moment, He was fused into my being, and I am no longer separate from

Him but am one with Him. He is in me and I in Him, each a part of the other.

Therefore I am literally thinking His thoughts, walking His steps, doing His works, breathing His breath. And, potentially (oh, that it might be ours experimentally), *all* His fullness dwells in me.

Not only is His righteousness mine, but His power, attributes, virtues and even His faith are all mine too as I daily live, drawing on His sustenance.

My faith is not directed toward Him as though He were removed into space, but I live on His faith here and now. Not by faith in the Son of God, but by *the* faith *of* the Son of God.

Fear not if your faith as you have experienced it thus far is limited and weak. Just as water poured into a glass takes the form of the glass, so does this faith take our form. It starts where we are. Believe that His faith is yours. Appropriate what you have. Start from there and believe in a big way in a big God. Faith is not believing God *can*, faith is believing God *will*.

CHAPTER 3

IF IT BE THY WILL

Let me again ask you to re-examine your concept of prayer and be ready to open your mind to possible new truths.

The following statement, while opposed to what many believe, is in effect the key to this entire book:

No prayer, to be a perfect prayer of faith, can contain the expression: *if it be thy will!* (To pray "if it be thy will," is quite different from "Thy will be done.")

There are many different kinds of prayer, prayers of thanksgiving, praise, confession, etc. We are now dealing with the prayer of faith, the prayer that God is constrained to answer, the prayer that literally ties the hands of God and that He *must* answer because His word is at stake. His name and honor stand behind His promises. When they are understood, claimed in faith, and presented at the throne room of heaven as a promissory note to be cashed, He must, He will answer.

The secret is to discern the will of God *ahead of time*, before you attempt to pray the prayer of faith. For if you do not know His will in a particular matter, you certainly cannot pray in faith for it to happen. But when you are confident of His will, offer the prayer of faith and it will be answered.

God beseeches His children, even reasons with them, to come often and *boldly* to Him. He says, "Of the works concerning my hands command ye me" (Isaiah 45:11). What an invitation! What potential! But is there one among us who dares pray that way? We can, when we know that what we pray for is within the scope of His will.

Often we begin our prayer boldly only to end with, "if it be thy will." In other words, "If You were going to do it anyway, Lord, go ahead and do it but leave me out of it." I can imagine that many times God hears the prayers and sees the faith of His children and prepares to open the fountain of heaven's blessings only to hear us finish our prayer, "if you were going to do it anyway." Then God must surely close the door of blessings and say to the Holy Spirit, "Put them all back, they don't really believe Me, they're just going through the motion of prayer."

If is the weakest word in the world. Does it denote faith, bold positive assurance, dynamic expectancy that must surely thrill the heart of God? Or does it show doubt, hesitation and uncertainty?

Many wonderful prayers have gone unanswered because they were rendered powerless with the word "if" in the middle of them.

When Jesus prayed, "Not my will but thine be done," in the Garden of Gethsemane, was He trying to teach us to pray in faith? Was He trying to find His Father's will? No, He was trying to submit His will to that of the Father. It was one last struggle of the flesh against the spirit.

In James 4:15 we read: "For that ye ought to say, If the Lord will, we shall live, and do this, or that."

Was James trying to teach them to pray in faith or was he reprimanding worldly Christians?

When Jesus taught His disciples to pray, "Thy will be done," did He say, "if it be thy will"? No, He did not.

Why then do so many prayers contain the phrase that drains the power from a prayer of faith? Because we have heard others do it so long we are in a rut. How often have you heard your pastor call on a man to pray for the offering only to hear him respond with the customary, "Lord, if it be Thy will, bless this offering"? Now, wait a minute. You and I know and the man knows that it *is* God's will to bless the offering. So why does he pray that way? Because he's heard it all of his life.

I have heard another person pray, "Lord, if it be Thy will, bless this service." Listen, if it isn't God's will to bless the service, fire the preacher, lock the doors, disband the church and forget it! But we know that it *is* God's will to bless that church and that service. Then why pray that way? Tradition.

The real reason however is probably this: We do not really believe that God is going to do anything so we have an easy way out in case He doesn't—an escape clause in fine print.

We go on and on with powerless service and unanswered prayer behind the excuse that it just must not have been God's will. In reality it was not His fault. It was His will but we had no faith, and because we did not believe, God had no one with whom to cooperate to accomplish His will.

We have the mistaken idea that God's will is always done. But such is not the case. Jesus went to His own village to do miracles of blessing and healing and save those who would believe. But "He did not many mighty works there because of their unbelief." (Matthew 13:58)

God gets blamed for many things that are not His will at all. We hear of a plane crash taking scores of lives and say, "Well, it just must have been the will of God," when perhaps the reason was not the will of God but the carelessness of man. God's will was not done there.

Then, too, it is important to note that just because something is God's will does not necessarily mean that it will happen. We are to find His will, cooperate with Him by positive activated faith, and then His will can be done.

Having the kind of faith that requires an escape clause, "if it be thy will," we can be sure that little that we've prayed for will happen. Suppose you are called upon to lead in prayer in an evangelistic service. You know that there are ten men present who have not as yet believed on the Saviour. As you begin to speak, you pray, "Lord, we are trusting You to save these men tonight. We believe You are going to do it. Thank You that they are all going to come and profess their faith in Thee tonight." Then you begin to think. *Now wait, what if they don't come tonight. I'll look kind of silly, won't I? Someone might come up and say, "What's the matter with your prayers? You prayed and they didn't come, did they?"*

So as an easy out you pray, "Lord, if it be thy will, save them." In other words, "Lord, if you were going to do it anyway, go ahead and do it, it's all right by me, but Lord leave me out of it, just forget about what I said a minute ago."

You need never pray, "If it be Thy will, save some particular one." There are some things in which we do not know His will and must give careful attention to discern it. But in most things we already know His will. And this truth is one in which we do, for God is

> not willing that any should perish, but that all men should come to repentance (II Peter 3:9).
>
> I exhort therefore, that, first of all, supplications, prayers, intercessions and giving of thanks, be made for all men; . . . For this is good and acceptable in the sight of God our Saviour; who will have all men to be saved, and to come unto the knowledge of the truth (I Timothy 2:1-4).

Remember this and learn it well. It can change your life.

You need never ask God, if it be His will to save your wife, your husband, your child, your friend. It is His will. But it may not be done because of sin, faithlessness, or unbelief. I believe that if the perfect will of God were done, every unconverted person on the earth would turn to Christ by faith in the next second. God permits men to choose against Him, to reject His offer of forgiveness and mercy, but He certainly does not will it. His perfect will is that all men be saved, although that will obviously is not done. So do not ask God again to save that dear one. Rather, go to your knees and begin to affirm, to believe, to receive. Thank God that He is going to save them. And if you do not really believe that He is going to, thank Him over and over again until you do believe it; soon you will begin to believe.

Positive thinking or positive praying can never save one single lost soul. But, oh, how those who already believe need to learn the art of positive living, thinking, believing, and praying. For what else does Paul mean when he says, "Whatsoever things are true, whatsoever things are honest, whatsover things are just, whatsoever things are pure, whatsoever things are lovely, whatsoever things are of good report, if there be any virtue, and if there be any praise, think on these things" (Philippians 4:8).

Recently, one of the nation's leading insurance salesmen made a phonograph record describing his philosophy of modern sales success. Everything he said was good, but it could have been said in one statement. "As he thinketh in his heart, so is he" (Proverbs 23:7). As I fix in my mind and heart the image of the thing for which I am praying, everything in my life begins to gravitate toward the accomplishment of it. It is seeing with the eye of faith.

"Now faith is the substance of things hoped for, the evidence of things not seen" (Hebrews 11:1).

In Springfield, Missouri, a lady asked that I pray for the conversion of her husband. I inquired if she were praying and learned that she had been doing so for thirty-five years. I was discouraged. Apparently I could not expect much help from her. She hadn't been getting very far. I asked her if she prayed, "If it be Thy will, save my husband"? She replied that she did. When I asked her why, she said she did not want God to do anything He didn't want to do. I told her that she didn't need to protect God, and showed her from the Bible that God's will was to save not only her husband but all men, and that it was her place to cooperate with God by believing Him and praying in faith, and that if she would promise never again to ask God to save her husband, I would pray with her. I suggested that she go home and spend an hour on her knees thanking God that

He was going to save him. She promised to try it. That night she came down the aisle to tell me of the thrill of praying in faith and when she turned to be seated, there was her husband. He had come to commit his life to the Master. One hour of praying in faith, believing, had done more good than thirty-five years of endless repetition and doubting hesitation!

How many churches have waited to build until the money was secure in the bank? How often have we waited for God to give the increase before we were willing to make the preparation? The prayer life, as the whole of Christian experience, is one of trust that claims the victory in advance. For we walk by faith, not by sight.

When my daughter Melodye Jan came to me at the age of five and asked for a doll house, I promised to build one and went back to reading an engrossing book. Soon I glanced out of the study window and saw her with her arms filled with dishes, toys, and dolls, making her little pilgrimage to the corner of the yard, where by now she had gathered a great pile of playthings. I asked my wife what the purpose of that impossible pile could be. "Oh, you promised her a doll house," she replied, "and she believes you. She's just getting ready for it." You would have thought I'd been hit by an atom bomb. I threw aside that book, raced to the lumber yard for supplies, and quickly built that little girl a doll house. Now why did I respond? Because she wanted it? No. Because she deserved it? No. Her daddy had given his word and she believed it and acted upon it. When I saw her faith, nothing could keep me from carrying out my word.

Suppose that after I had promised, she had kept coming and asking, "Are you sure you really mean it? You won't forget will you? I haven't seen **any** doll house around here," over and over again. I would probably have become disgusted at her lack of faith in my promised word and, disappointed at her doubts, would have just forgotten the whole thing. But she didn't doubt. She didn't question. I had revealed my will, given my word, and she was willing to believe, accept, and act.

Were you to hire an employee to do a job and then continually check up for fear that he was not doing it, it would certainly be obvious that you did not trust him. If you ask God for something and then set out to make other provision for accomplishing it, it is likewise obvious that you have not really prayed in faith and do not really trust Him.

Let us take God at His word and pray, believe, and act in positive faith, and God will surely build our spiritual doll houses.

Charles Haddon Spurgeon, a great preacher of the 1800's, had just finished lecturing to his students on the call to the ministry, when a young ministerial student approached him. "Doctor Spurgeon, you said that one sign of God's call is His blessing us with results when we preach. I've been preaching for two and a half years and haven't had a convert yet. I think I'm going to quit."

With years of experience and wisdom and a saintly twinkle in his eye, the old minister said, "Well, young whippersnapper, who do you think you are anyway? You don't expect someone to be saved every time you preach now do you?"

"Well, no sir," stammered the boy, "I guess not."

"Then that," replied the great preacher, "Is the very reason they're not."

Think about it. This is an awfully big world and

God must surely be very busy with all the endless duties of ordering our lives. Do you really expect God to stop what He's doing and answer your every prayer? Haven't you prayed so often with no answer that it is more or less just a ritual? Well, do you expect God to answer? No? That is exactly the reason He doesn't!

CHAPTER 4

THE WILL OF GOD

Answered prayer entails the meeting of two must factors. One, my faith to believe, and two, God's willingness to bestow. Now the prime concern becomes, how may I know His will?

The essential characteristic of the fall of man was that of independent action apart from the revealed will of God. Since then the problem of knowing the will of God has always been of concern to man. One can live by either of two philosophies. Will I guide my life by what *I will*, what I desire, what I want? But Christianity is a cross, and a cross is "I" crossed out. Then I must, live by the alternate philosophy, "Thy will be done."

Man in his original image of God was endowed with three capacities for knowing the Father—knowledge, emotion, and will. Man distanced from God by sin did not lose these capacities, but he did lose their true sphere of exercise.

His intellect, now darkened will only see things that are near. He will ask, "How can it be? For what purpose is this?" Man's emotion is deadened and will attempt to satisfy itself on things material rather than eternal. His will, degraded, will ever attempt to be masterful rather than submissive.

Once man had perfect knowledge of the will of God, but now he must seek to know His will through a power higher than himself.

To begin with, it is essential to realize that God is more willing for you to know His will than you are to know it. Your Heavenly Father is not playing spiritual cat and mouse with you. Many believe that God's will is a hidden mystery that we must set out to discover, when in reality we must open our hearts to the evident will of God. Remember that God wants you to know His will and is doing everything that He can to make it obvious to you. It is not some deep mystery that God does not want us to find. God wants only the best for His own, and your knowledge of His perfect will is the best.

The will of God will usually be revealed to you through normal means where possible to do so. Don't look for a Damascus road experience. God had to speak to the Apostle Paul in that way because his heart was hardened against the will of God and he had no desire to know God's will. Many times the will of God is obvious. So do not expect it to be made known to you through a supernatural means.

Normally guidance will come one step at a time. We are easily frustrated because we do not know what God would have of us in twenty years, when in reality if we did know, it would only serve to confuse. God will guide you step by step. You need not know about tomorrow as long as you walk in the light you have today. Don't live in the future. "Sufficient unto the day is the evil thereof" (Matthew 6:34).

God will always reveal His will in time for you to prepare for it. Many live in a constant fear that God will spring on them some great task for which they are totally unprepared.

Sometimes guidance comes unsought. Allow me to share with you a personal experience. Before God called me to preach, I served in the capacity of a Christian minister of music. One night after I had finished conducting the music service, a stranger walked up to me and said, "Have you ever felt that God might be calling you to preach?" and walked off. Needless to say, it made quite an impression on me. Even more important to me was that it happened three times with three different people. I have no doubts that God spoke to me through them.

While the will of God is not always pleasant immediately, it will be pleasant and desirable in the long run. It is incorrect to assume that if something is not pleasant, it is not the will of God. The refiner's fire is never pleasant to the gold. The operation is never pleasant to the patient. However, in the overall effect, it is not only desirable but pleasant in its results. Examine for a moment Romans 8:28: "For we know that all things work together for good to them that love God, to them who are the called according to his purpose." We emphasize the *all things* and think that all things are desirable and good and miss the point entirely. God is not stressing that *all things* are good but that all things *work together* for good.

Remember when women used to make cakes—before the modern day of mixes in a box? Grandma's chocolate cake had to contain some mighty bitter chocolate, some mighty salty salt, and some mighty powerful soda. How would you like to eat some of that chocolate by itself or some soda or salt alone?

On the other hand, how would a chocolate cake be without the chocolate or the soda or the salt? The salt and soda of everyday life are not always pleasant, but all things must work together for the total good of a life worth living.

Chapter 5

THE GREAT DISCOVERY

Yes, you may now begin to change your entire life. You can enter into a state of constant abiding in Christ, with powerful answers to positive prayers, that you may have never known before because you can know God's will unquestionably and pray unhesitatingly. The first step in knowing the will of God lies in being willing to do His will when you know it. Read again John 7:17: "If any man will do his will, he shall know the doctrine, whether it be of God, or whether I speak of myself."

For three years Jesus had been trying to convince the Jews that He was the Son of God but had apparently failed. Finally He turned to them and said the reason you do not know whether I am the Son and whether my doctrine is God's, is that you would not be willing to accept me if I were God's Son. He said that you must be willing to accept me or you shall never know. In other words, even if you did know I were the Son of God, even if you were convinced, you would never admit it because your unwilling hearts are not open to the truth.

God will never impose the revelation of His will upon your already predetermined will. Remember, I said earlier that to pray "if it be Thy will" and "Thy will be done" are two entirely different things. If you already know God's will, obviously you do not need to pray "if it be Thy will." However, if you do not know His will, the very first step is to have a willing mind and a willing heart. Then begin by praying, "Thy will be done." You must submit your will to that of the Father before He will reveal His will to you. Do not many of us pray with this kind of attitude: "Lord, this is what I want, now let's hear what you have to say"? But you can never come to God this way. A willingness to do His will when He reveals it is the basic requirement for knowing that will.

Many of you have probably been thinking about the matter of praying for the sick and wondering about, "if it be Thy will," when praying for them. If your only desire is to discharge your responsibility by going from hospital to hospital, and praying over loved ones and friends, "If it be Thy will, heal this one," you may be satisfied with meager results. But to the one who would pray sincerely and intelligently I suggest a more realistic approach. Before you pray that God will heal that person, go to God with a willing heart and ask Him to make you receptive to the knowledge of His will. As you wait, perhaps God will say, "No, my child, this is not within the scope of my will. I do not ordain healing in this particular case; this illness is for a purpose," and then you can only pray "Yes, Lord, Thy will be done" and do not offer the prayer of faith for that person's healing. God can speak this directly to our hearts.

I hear someone say, "Then what can I pray at the bed of a loved one?" You can pray that he will have the grace and courage to bear his illness to the glory of God. You can pray that God will relieve his suffering. You can pray that through his illness much permanent good may come as he witnesses for Christ to doctors, nurses, and friends. You can pray that many might be impressed with his courage and faith and be brought to know the God that gives courage and sustains the faithful in seasons of physical illness.

A woman asked once that I pray for her son who was in college, that he might know God's will for his life, because he was anxious to find out whether it was something that he wanted to do or not. Both she and her son were wasting their time. We cannot tell God what we want and then try to fit Him into our plans.

Regarding guidance, I do not believe that God desires the same thing for every minister. He will direct some to have a college education; others, seminary and doctoral work. At one time in my life I had a good deal of difficulty finding His will in this matter. I had college and a bit of seminary training, but did not want to finish seminary. I didn't particularly care whether God wanted me to go or not. I simply did not want to finish. All the while I prayed, "Lord, what do You want me to do? But I hope it isn't going to seminary." I could never find His will.

Then I decided I did want to go. I did not particularly seek God's mind in the matter but rather made up my own mind that I was going. I attempted to sell my home, buy another near the seminary and move. I enrolled in classes, made my plans accordingly and kept on praying, "Lord, I hope it's all right because now I've decided I'm going." Still I was not certain. This was the most miserable experience of my life, not knowing for certain that I was right but doing it because I half-heartedly felt that I should. Finally, in a moment of surrender I honestly came to the place that I did not care one way or the other and prayed, "Lord, Thy will be done." In thirty seconds, I knew God's will and have never doubted that decision since.

One of the easiest things in the world for me now, is to learn the will of God in my life. The reason is simple. I have come to the place that in everything I can say, "For better or worse, for richer or poorer, missionary, pastor, evangelist, big church or small, I have no desire for my own life, but am perfectly willing to do the will of God."

The second (as well as the third) way that one may know the will of God lies hidden in an oft-quoted but little-understood passage from the Bible. Listen closely to this treasure from Romans, chapter 12, verses 1 and 2:

> I beseech you therefore, brethren, by the mercies of God, that ye present your bodies a living sacrifice, holy, acceptable unto God, which is your reasonable service. And be not conformed to this world: but be ye transformed by the renewing of your mind, that ye may prove what is that good, and acceptable, and perfect, will of God.

We preach much about separation and consecration from this verse. But look at it again. What does it really say? The great apostle sets forth two key ways to know the will of God, for when he says "that ye may prove," the literal meaning is "that ye may know that good and acceptable and perfect will of God." The first factor is a holy, sacrificial body. At first glance it may seem that the actual physical body of the believer is not inferred, but it is. The Bible has much to say about the body. The spiritual condition of a Christian is often closely related to his physical condition. Paul, in the Bible, says, "Your body is the temple of the Holy Ghost" (I Corinthians 6:19); and "I keep under my body" (I Corinthians 9:27), for the relationship of the body to the soul is unfathomable. If you would sincerely know the will of God, first offer your body as a living sacrifice. Do all within your power to present your physical body the best possible specimen to God, keeping your body fit by eating properly, getting plenty of exercise and sleep, and avoiding tobacco and alcohol. Offering your body as a living sacrifice also includes the careful training of a keen mind, an alert brain, a well-guarded tongue, and consecrated ears and eyes that hear and see only that which brings glory to the Father.

Next he says "Be not conformed to this world." Christian young person, be not conformed to this world and you shall know the will of God. It is absolutely impossible for a careless, worldly Christian to discern the keener things of God's will.

Third, you can know the will of God through the Word of God. Don't toss this aside and say "I've heard it before." Of course, you have always known the Bible was a faithful guide and that God spoke to us through His Word. But let me point out two important factors that perhaps you have not thought of in knowing God's will from His Word. The first is this. God's Word is not a book of laws and rules, but where laws and rules are found they are to be observed and obeyed, for His Word does not change. Basically the Bible is a book of principles. Read again the Sermon on the Mount from Matthew 5, 6, and 7. Jesus said adultery is a sin and, though He did not change that law, He did add that the impure thought is just as great a sin (Matthew 5:28). He said that murder was wrong and carried a great penalty, but added that hatred in the heart that produces murder is equally wrong. The Bible does not say, "Thou shalt not smoke." But the principle there that tells me to care for my body covers many things. It does not say, "Thou shalt do fifty pushups a day," but it does say to care for my body. So remember that when seeking to know God's will from God's Word, we find it through general teachings and principles taught in His Word where direct commandments and teachings are not made.

Furthermore, in seeking to know God's will through the Word of God, remember His Word does not change. Some people pray about things that God has already made clear, hoping against hope that He will answer them according to their desires. But God will never change His Word. The teaching of the Word of God is that we ought to seek Him early in the day when our minds are the keenest. Someone says, "I will pray about it. I will think about it." You don't have to think about it. Just get up. God says do it. A farmer in a little western Oklahoma town asked that I pray with him about tithing. I told him that I would not for God has told us it is His will that we give Him one day of seven and one dollar of ten, thousands of years ago and He will not tell us something different today.

God will not tell you anything different today than He has already told you in His Word. If the Bible is clear on a particular matter you needn't pray about it. Just do it. Don't try to take one verse of Scripture to justify your particular desire or opinion when it is against the plain teaching of the majority of Scriptures in the Bible. His Word changeth not.

The fourth way you may know the will of God is by circumstances or "open doors." The person who is honestly seeking to find the will of the Lord can see the hand of God in many ways. A young person is about to enter college. Three possibilities are before him, but he does not know which to pursue. College "A" is more expensive than the others, but he plans to save on expenses by staying with an aunt. College "B" has a higher scholastic standard than he had expected and he finds himself unable to go. In the meantime the aunt moves and the door is closed at College "A." At College "C" he has both the means and the scholastic standing to enroll. Which college should he choose? The answer is obvious. We can follow the leadership of God step by step in the way things providentially work out if we are seeking to know His will and daily asking for guidance as He opens the doors.

The fifth way to know God's will is by submission to the Holy Spirit. The Apostle Paul tells us to present our bodies. To whom are they to be presented? God, the Father? But He is in Heaven. Christ the Son? But then he has returned to the Father and is not now on earth. Surely he does not need a body. It is to the Holy Spirit that we yield our members as vessels for His service. To many of us, the Holy Spirit is a stranger. We pray, "God, send the Holy Spirit," or "Lord, please let the Holy Spirit do this or that," when in reality we need not go by way of Heaven and back to earth at all. The Holy Spirit is here. He is in you. He guides and teaches you, when you have yielded your heart to Christ by faith. You can know Him, you can have constant fellowship with Him. Over and over the Bible tells us that the

Holy Spirit spoke definite words of leadership and direction to men of the Old and New Testaments. Over two thousand times the Bible says "Thus saith the Holy Ghost." If the Holy Spirit can speak to me, why can I not speak to Him? Try it. Bow your head and say, "Holy Spirit, I know Thou art indwelling me. I know that Jesus has risen and ascended to heaven and I know that Thou art come to be my constant companion and guide. I pray Thee, speak to me and guide me now." His purpose is to lead you and teach you. Ask Him to do it.

We may know the will of God by our own common sense. You can sit down and figure out many things for yourself. You may say, "that isn't being spiritual." But who do you think gave you those brains to figure with? Who gave you the ability to reason, to discern, to think? It was God, was it not? Remember this principle. God will never reveal His will to you in some special way if at birth He has already equipped you with the faculties to know His will. You would not glorify God by standing on the street corner and praying for Him to tell you what time it is, if He has given you eyes with which to see, money enough to buy a wrist watch and intelligence enough to tell time. Don't pray about it. Just look at your watch. If your church is in an evangelistic endeavor and you meet an unsaved friend on the street, you need not pray about witnessing to him and inviting him to church. Just do it. Your common sense will dictate that. If the light is red, don't pray about stopping. Stop. If it is green, don't pray about going. Go. If God has equipped you with the physical abilities to learn His will, it will not come to you in a special way.

Finally and most important of all you *will* know the will of God when you know God.

Examine the word *know*. It is a precious word and has the deepest meaning for the Christian. The Apostle Paul had a desire to live a life of constant fellowship with the Father. He wanted his desires, his ambitions, his will to cease to exist. He literally wished that Paul might die and rise spiritually—a new life, totally yielded to that of the Father—that he might experience the bliss that was his, potentially, in being in complete oneness with Christ. He said that he lived his life by the faith of the Son of God, that the life of Jesus was his life, and he literally lived by His person. To enter into the state of resurrection oneness with Christ, he must be resurrected spiritually and so, first must die. To die like this, he said, "I must know him."

When Mary was told by the angel that she was to give birth to the holy child Jesus, she said, "How shall this be, seeing I know not a man?" (Luke 1:34). In the Old Testament, we find the words, "Adam knew Eve his wife; and she conceived, and bare Cain" (Genesis 4:1). The same word is used when Paul said "That I might know him and the power of his resurrection" (Philippians 3:10). Know obviously means, "to be in union with."

The relationship of the believer to Christ is compared in the Bible with the relationship that exists between a husband and wife. When a man and woman marry they have the same name, the same bank account, the same possessions. That which belongs to one is common to both. Legally, they are one. Emotionally, physically, mentally, spiritually in the ideal state of wedded union, they are one. Paul's prayer is that he would enter into this same kind of

39

union with Christ.

Have you ever known a couple, perhaps your parents or grandparents who have been married for forty, fifty, even sixty years, who talked alike, acted alike, thought alike and even looked alike? They have been together for so long that the desires and actions of the two individuals have been melted into perfect unity. Ask one what the other likes, thinks, or believes and he will know. Were you to ask me if my wife likes hats, I wouldn't have to ask her, I already know. I know her that well. Through constant fellowship and daily communion with God, we can know how God thinks, what He desires, and what He wills because we know Him.

A boy marries his sweetheart. They consecrate the marriage vows, but he immediately leaves for Africa and she for Japan. Every day for fifty years they write each other their every waking thought and action. What will happen? They will know everything there is possible to know *about* each other, but they will not *know* each other.

To know someone, you must spend time with that person. You can go to every college and seminary on earth. You can take every course offered. You can memorize the Bible. You can master theology in every language known to man. You can know all that the finite mind will ever know *about* God, but you will never *know* God until you learn to spend time in prayer *with* Him. There is no exception. Power with God, power to know the will of God, power in positive prayer that brings definite results, comes only through much time daily in prayer with God.

But if most of us were honest, I feel that we would have to admit that we have never learned to pray for very long at a time. I know that the Bible says we are not heard for our much speaking, and isn't that a good excuse not to pray? Wouldn't most of us be embarrassed if we were called on to pray for ten minutes by the clock? Wouldn't we just run out of things to say? Don't most of us pray "Dear Lord, thank You for Your blessings. Bless the missionaries. Forgive me of my sins," and that exhausts our supply of prayer material? Take heart, you can learn to spend time in prayer with God.

In the following chapters, we will consider the actual steps of prayer, what to say and how to say it— how to build a framework upon which to construct a substantial prayer life that will acquaint you with God, that will lead to the joy that comes from knowing God through much time in prayer with Him.

CHAPTER 6

PRAISE THE LORD

Before we begin the actual mechanics of prayer, allow me to share with you an important factor that begins even before you pray. You must do everything physically possible to get alone with God. It is difficult to pray with all your heart in front of others, and almost impossible to pray an unaffected prayer in a church service. One cannot help but be conscious of external surroundings, particularly the ears of other people. Personally, I am afraid that I am guilty much of the time of praying *to* people and *for* people rather than God when I pray publicly.

Three things should help you get alone with God. The first is physical solitude. Get away from people and things. Many times you will have to go into another room, pull down the blinds, and lock the door to find quietness for meditation. If you are tempted to look around, bury your head in a pillow. Place cotton in your ears. By shutting out sound and sight you will find it easier to be shut in with God.

Second, have the same place to pray all the time. Select a chair, a corner of the bed, a certain spot in the room, and find a comfortable position. (Perhaps pillows under your knees will make prayer more inviting. There is no "piosity" in being uncomfortable when you pray.) Go to the same place at the same time in the same position every day, and prayer will become a habit, delightfully inviting and hard to break. Consistency is of the utmost necessity.

Third, before you begin to talk to God, whether audibly or in your heart, relax momentarily. Do not rush hurriedly into the presence of God. Take a few deep breaths. Let your mind be quiet and your body relaxed. Wait a moment that you might know the conscious presence of Him that said, "Be still, and know that I am God" (Psalm 46:10). I can imagine the children of Israel at the Red Sea, organizing their armies, excitedly maneuvering into position for the great venture. Suddenly Moses says, "Stand still, and see the salvation of the Lord" (Exodus 14:13). Learn to stand still a moment. In the old days if someone missed the stagecoach, he would wait five days for another. Today, if we have to wait three seconds in a revolving door, we have a heart attack. The spirit of the Lord moves upon peaceful waters. Get quiet before Him. Get alone with Him and know the reality of His presence.

Now you are ready to pray.

The first step of prayer is praise. It is important to note that I have placed praise first. You will find the confession of sin to be the third step. I would suggest that you do not begin your prayer with the confession of sin. Why do most of us do this? Probably because David said, "If I regard iniquity in my heart, the Lord will not hear me." But what did he mean? If I have any sin in my heart, God will not hear my prayer, therefore I must confess it first or God will not hear the rest of my prayer? No, he does not mean if I merely *have* iniquity in my heart. The word regard means retain; thus, if I *retain* iniquity in my heart; He will not hear me. If I covet some sin, if I harbor it in one corner of my heart, if I refuse to confess it, then God will not hear me. If we only prayed when there were no sins in our heart, I fear that we should never pray.

If you begin your prayer by confessing your sin, you will find yourself in a very unpleasant frame of mind, prayer will become distasteful and you will not be apt to pray for very long. Most of us need to do everything we can to make prayer desirable. The first thing you do in anything can make or break you—your first impression, your first thought, your first reaction. If a television program begins with soft music and a pathetic introduction, most men will turn it off. But let the bright lights flare, the trumpets blast and the curtain swing high and they will stay around to see what's going to happen next. You can make a bad impression and never recover from it, but you can start well and cover a multitude of wrongs. So it is in prayer. Begin on high. Start positively. Let your prayer begin by praising God and you will soon find yourself in a frame of mind such that you will not want to be torn from prayer at all.

Earlier I said that we need some positive thinking, positive believing and positive praying. The secret to salesmanship, the secret to life, the secret to success is thinking and believing positively. So it is in prayer. If you rise in the morning, look out the window and say, "Oh what a miserable day, everything's going wrong today," you won't be disappointed. It will. But if you can begin your day with, "Praise God, what a wonderful privilege to be alive," and think good thoughts—think on things lovely, pure, virtuous, things of good report—you will indeed have a good day.

Have you ever met a Christian that you really liked to be around? Someone that seemed to have magnetic attraction to other people? That person has probably learned the secret of praising the Lord. Many folks go around with a sour attitude toward life and an expression on their face that looks as though they had been weaned on dill pickles. But some people seem to have a verve, a vitality, a zest for living. They have learned the secret of praising God. When you have learned this, you will have learned the secret of one of the most satisfying experiences of life.

It takes over fifty face muscles to frown, but only sixteen to smile. I don't know what He did for you, but when God changed my life through personal faith in Christ, He put a spring in my step, a song in my heart, a smile on my face, and gave me a zest for living.

Sit down with at least two other people and slowly say "Praise the Lord" ten times. If you don't have a smile on your face by the end of that, you will probably never smile at anything. It is impossible to say "Praise the Lord" and frown. Try it! It just won't come out.

Someone is probably thinking, "This is well and good, but how do I praise the Lord at the beginning of my prayer? Do I just start saying Praise the Lord, Praise the Lord, over and over again?" No. There are three very wonderful ways that you can praise the Lord—in your own words, with Psalms, and with music.

To praise God is simply to brag on the Lord. Mary said, "My soul doth magnify the Lord" (Luke 1:46). The psalmist said, "My soul shall make her boast in the Lord: the humble shall hear thereof, and be glad" (Psalm 34:2). How would you define boast? Is there any better definition than bragging? That's what praising the Lord is—bragging on Jesus.

There are many things about the nature of God that I do not understand but that I accept. One of them is that there is something about the nature of God that demands praise. What do you think of when you think of magnifying the Lord? To magnify means to increase out of true proportion. Were you to brag on me or were I to brag on you, we could lie about each other and exalt ourselves out of every proper proportion, but when you praise the Lord, you are on safe ground. You cannot say too much about God. So first of all, tell the Lord how great He is. Tell Him in your own words what you think of Him in all His greatness. You would not have difficulty bragging on a loved one or a friend. Think of the greatness and goodness of a majestic God and praise Him for every facet of His personality and mighty works that the Spirit of God brings to your mind.

Next, praise God through the Psalms. You can turn almost anywhere in the Psalms and find a passage that will aid you in praising God. As you are on your knees before God, open your Bible and turn at random through this song book of the Bible. Pick out a good verse. Read it aloud. Read it again. Memorize it. Look up and say it to God. Make it your own. Say it in your own words. Repeat it over and over. It will suggest other things. The Psalms are a great primer for the pump that wells up in fountains of praise to the Lord.

The third and best way, perhaps, is to praise God through music; not in the choir, or in the church, but right there on your knees. If you can sing, sing. If not, say the words. If you want to sing out loud, do so. If to yourself, do that. Many wonderful songs will rise forth from the heart of the soul that is striving to praise God. Pray these songs over in your heart. Say the words of "Revive Us Again." "We praise Thee, O God! for the Son of Thy love, For Jesus who died, and is now gone above." Think about the words.

"We praise Thee, O God! for the Son of Thy love." This means that Jesus was not born of the will of man, or of the will of the flesh, but He was literally the result, the product, the fruit, the Son of God's love, born from the heart of a God who loves mankind so much that the inevitable response of His love was Jesus, His Son. Then continue "For Jesus who died, and is now gone above." Praise Him for His death, His resurrection, His ascension, His intercession, His coming return. This will suggest innumerable other things for which to praise Him, such as His miracles, His grace, His mercy, the home He is preparing in heaven, His Book, His blood.

The next verse begins, "We praise Thee, O God! for Thy spirit of light, Who has shown us our Saviour, and scattered our night." What does it mean? Had not the Holy Spirit come and scattered the night of sin and revealed Christ to our hearts, we could not have been saved. You will think of praising Him for your own personal experience with Christ, His Son, and the inevitable will follow, "Hallelujah! Thine the glory, Hallelujah! amen."

There are many other wonderful songs. "Praise Him! praise Him! Jesus, our blessed Redeemer! Sing, O Earth, His wonderful love proclaim! Hail Him! hail Him! highest archangels in glory; Strength and honor give to His holy name!"

CHAPTER 7

THANKSGIVING

The second step in prayer is thanksgiving. I mentioned that there were some things about the nature of God that we do not understand. We do understand, however, that God appreciates the heartfelt prayers of grateful children. Perhaps the greatest sin of omission in the United States is the sin of thanklessness.

Examine Psalm 100:4, "Enter into his gates with thanksgiving, and into his courts with praise: be thankful unto him, and bless his name." The psalmist speaks of two different steps in prayer. There is not only praising Him and blessing His name but also an attitude of thankfulness and an act of thanksgiving. While praising God is of the utmost importance, thanking God is another great privilege of the child of God.

This psalm carries with it the idea of a kingdom and a palace. In ancient times the king lived in a beautiful palace surrounded by a courtyard with court walls. Beyond this lay the city walls and the gates. Into the gates of the city came the merchants, travelers, and all who were at peace with the king. Articles were traded; business services rendered. The market place was there and all the commoners were welcomed. To enter into a personal audience with the king, however, one had to pass through the court wall, into the courtyard, and then into the presence of the king.

We have national holidays set aside for thanksgiving, but to enter into a personal relationship with the King one must go a step farther inside to His courts. This is done by praising the Lord. And so as we begin our prayers by praising God, we go a step farther into the intimacy of His presence beyond what thanksgiving can do.

Suppose you invited a friend for dinner, and upon leaving he thanked you for your hospitality? This would be expected. But wouldn't it be more personal, more meaningful, if he began to brag on you, to praise you, to compliment you for your home, your neatness, your warmth? Praising God is going the second step.

Yet, thanking God is not only the privilege and responsibility, but the desire of every grateful heart. Naturally, all of us are grateful for the blessings of God, but expressing them verbally, not only blesses the great heart of God, but blesses our hearts, too. Some time ago as my wife was holding our little son, Timmy, she remarked, "Isn't it wonderful to be able to read in his eyes the love and appreciation that is there for our just being his mother and daddy." I knew what she meant and was not surprised when she added, "But wouldn't it be wonderful if we could just hear him say it?"

I fear that the number of those among us who return to thank God is very small in comparison with the multitude that find it so easy to make our requests known to Him. Thanks should be offered not only for our personal blessings but for all of those wonderful things that we share with others. Thanksgiving for the sunshine, the beauties of creation and all our mutual blessings is never out of style. Thanking God is a great antidote for depression, doubting, and unpleasantness.

As you begin to thank God, pause for Him to remind you of every blessing. Two categories are helpful here—physical blessings and spiritual blessings. Perhaps nothing is as old and yet as relevant as the old adage "I complained because I had no shoes until I met a man who had no feet."

If you think that you have nothing for which to be thankful, name every physical blessing that you enjoy. Thank God for your health and the health of your family. Thank Him for the perfection of their bodies. You say, "But my child was born blind"; but some children are born dead. You can find much for which to thank God. Thank Him for your clothes, your home, your automobile, your possessions, your watch, your ring, your furniture, food in your cupboard and money in the bank. Perhaps you are thinking, "But I only have fifty dollars." There are some people who only have five dollars." Perhaps you do only have five dollars. There are many people around the world that would kill to get that amount.

Have you ever thanked Him for your everyday blessings, the things you take for granted the most? What about your refrigerator? This may seem strange to the modern-day housewife, but I have been in countries in which refrigerators are luxuries. In Ireland, for example, few if any of the hundreds of homes that we visited had refrigerators. When the Irish housewife wants something cold, she thinks no more of walking five or six blocks to the grocer's, who may be the only one in the community who can afford a refrigerator, than you think of walking five or six steps across your kitchen. Did you ever thank God for your bathtub? I have seen countries where people only bathe once every two or three weeks. Perhaps you wouldn't bathe either if you had to walk fifteen blocks to a public bathhouse and pay thirty-five cents for a bath and made only twenty dollars a week.

Have you ever thanked God for your automobile? Stop ten young men on the streets of the United States and ask and you will find that all ten of them can drive an automobile. Ask ten young men the same question in many other countries and only one in ten will know how to drive. Why learn to drive when you know that you will never be able to afford an automobile or thirty-five cent gasoline?

In the spring of 1959 we landed at the Belfast airport, and drove about twelve miles to downtown Belfast. We must have passed at least ten thousand people walking from the airport to town and another ten thousand on bicycles. Do you know what young people do on dates there? They ride bicycles. They take long walks in the afternoon. People in Belfast walk or ride bicycles to work. They would no more think of getting in an automobile to go six blocks than you would to go six feet. They just walk, walk, walk. Most of us have never thanked God for the automobile, radio, television, electrical appliances, dishwashers, telephones and all the other things we take for granted.

Also thank God for your spiritual blessings. Thank Him for Himself, for His Son—for His life, death, and resurrection. Thank Him for your own personal experience with Him, your own salvation. Thank Him for the Spirit of God that led you to Him. Thank Him for the one that He used to bring you to Himself. Thank God for your church—the building and every person in it. Thank Him for the musicians, the choir, teachers and deacons who serve long and faithfully. Thank God for your pastor, his wife and family. You will never know, for there is no way of explaining, what it means to be a minister of the Gospel. To be sure, the fruits are many and varied, but the pressures are often unspeakable.

I know of some men who receive twenty-five and fifty dollars a week for preaching the gospel, but if these same men were to turn their talents and efforts into secular work, they would make at least three times that amount. I know of other ministers who are serving churches of ten thousand members who make fifteen and twenty thousand dollars a year and who administer budgets of a million dollars annually. This may sound like a lot of money, but how much would a businessman earn that presided over a million-dollar concern with ten thousand people in his care? $10,000? $25,000? No, more like $100,-000. Many a minister has four years of high school, four years of college and three to five years of seminary. Few doctors or lawyers have more education or more internship than most ministers, but their income is normally five to ten times that of the minister.

The first few months after I entered the ministry I would go off to a new field to serve for a brief period of time in evangelistic service. I thoroughly enjoyed being on an expense account and would often glory in the nice room and the best steaks that I could buy. But soon I learned that someone had to pay the bill and that every brick and square yard of carpet in the church is there because someone who did not have to do so gave from a heart of love. I thank God for the faithfulness of many saints who over the years have made it possible for us to enjoy Christianity as we now know it. We would do well in memorizing and praying the opening verses of one of the best loved of all the Psalms, "Bless the Lord, O my soul: and all that is within me, bless his holy name. Bless the Lord, O my soul, and forget not all his benefits: who forgiveth all thine iniquities; who healeth all thy diseases; who redeemeth thy life from destruction; who crowneth thee with lovingkindness and tender mercies" (Psalm 103:1-4).

Chapter 8

SIN

We turn from the most desirable aspect of prayer to the unenjoyable but important aspect of confessing our sins.

First John 1:9 tells us: "If we confess our sins, he is faithful and just to forgive us our sins, and to cleanse us from all unrighteousness." Perhaps this verse is old-hat to you, but a careful study of each word will reveal some important truths regarding sin.

Note the word "If." The forgiveness of our sins is conditional, not automatic. It is conditional upon our repentance and confession. The next verse says, "If we say that we have not sinned, we make him a liar and his word is not in us." Every Christian is confronted with the task of confessing sins daily, for on this condition is the promise of forgiveness immediate.

The death of our *sins* is not automatic at the time of conversion, but forgiveness of *sin* is, for *sin* is a condition of the heart that produces these individual *sins*. To be sure, when one receives the Lord Jesus as his own personal Saviour the guilt of his sinful nature is made right with God and forgiven. However, we do not become perfect but do continue sinning and shall as long as we are in this mortal body.

What then was forgiven when I believed on the Lord Jesus Christ? Was it the presence of my sin? No, I *will* be saved from sin's presence, but now I must live in a world of sin. Was it the power of sin? Potentially, yes, for I am daily being saved from sin's power as I grow in grace.

But that from which I was saved instantaneously was the *guilt* of my sin. I shall never be called into condemnation for it, for in one act of faith I was freed from sin's condemnation when I accepted God's gracious provision of His Son. I am in a state of righteousness before God because I once confessed the fact that I was a sinner by nature and that my heart was one of sin.

David said, "Behold, I was shapen in iniquity; and in sin did my mother conceive me" (Psalm 51:5). He means simply that from the very moment of conception, the principle of sin was present and therefore I too am a sinner in my innermost being. You can see the principle of sin developing in the smallest child. Put a young child in a playpen with other children and before he can walk or talk, he will not only refuse to give his toys away, but will selfishly grab for the toys of his playmates. This child is too young to sin, but the principle of sin, the seed of sin, is alive and flourishing in his being; and he will, one day, commit sins because the seed of sin is present.

The child of God who has been born again by a personal act of faith between himself and the Lord Jesus lives in a state of right relationship with God, and that relationship cannot be broken. However, the Christian also lives, in a state of fellowship which can easily be broken. When my children disobey me, they are corrected and do not receive the things they desire. This does not mean that they are no longer my children but rather that we are out of fellowship. The daily confession of our sins to God is not a condition of our relationship with Him, but rather of our fellowship.

To understand this further, it will help to realize that when one is converted he does not become perfect. God does not then and there eradicate the old nature of sin, else we should never sin again. Rather, at the instant of conversion God places into our being an entirely new nature, His own nature, and now we possess two natures—the old and the new, the carnal and the spiritual, the flesh and the spirit. Our gaining heaven is not determined by the victory of the struggle of these two natures. But our daily fellowship with God *is* affected. An old missionary returned to the home of a convert among the Mohave Indians. When the missionary asked him how he was doing, old Joe said, "Well, it seems that I have a black dog and a white dog inside of me and they are always fighting." The missionary asked him, "Which one wins?" and Joe said, "The one I feed the most." Our daily fellowship with God is determined by which nature we feed the most. And confessing our sins is an essential part of fellowship.

The next word in our verse is, "we." This pronoun refers to Christians, not merely to those who have joined the church, reformed, or done good works, but to those who have had a personal encounter with God through faith in His Son. First John was written by a Christian under the leadership of the Holy Spirit, about Christians and to Christians. It is *to Christians* that the promise of fellowship is held forth. Mark the words, "we," and "sins," for we Christians are to confess our sins. This means individually to enumerate, name, repent of, and forsake our sins. Many people have tried to find peace of mind and forgiveness in the philosophies of Jesus without first receiving Him personally. To be a Christian is not to accept and know His teachings, it is to know Him. For the unconverted to confess his *sins*, is useless. His need is to confess his *sin*, to confess the fact that he is a sinner by nature, that his very being is one of sin and that he is totally dead and apart from God.

With the Christian however, it is not a matter of *sin*, but *sins*. The promise to the Christian is not that he confess his sin for forgiveness, for he has already done that in one act of repentance and faith. It is that he confess his sins, sins which are the result of that old nature of sin that is present until death, that is forgiven but not eradicated.

I wonder what would be our reaction if we knew how many sins were piled up between ourselves and God because we have never learned that we are to confess sins individually. It may be that you have not been in perfect fellowship with God, not had every sin forgiven, for many many months and years. Asking God daily to forgive our sins in general is not enough. Perhaps it seems that you cannot remember each of your sins and fear that there are some that are unforgiven that you have not remembered. Often we pray "Lord, forgive me of the sins I have committed and those things that were wrong that I did not know were sins," but you need not do this if you will wait patiently before the Lord. He will certainly bring them to your memory and place the gentle finger of His convicting spirit upon them.

The word "confess" is an important one.

To confess with Bible confession does not merely mean to tell. It also means to change. If I were to go to the newspaper, buy a full-page ad, and publicly admit to the world every sin and wrong that I have ever done and continue doing them, it would surely be to no avail. God knows every sin we have committed. He knows them before we do them. Why then does He require that I tell Him what He already knows? It is not just to be telling God but rather, to change my attitude about them and, having changed my attitude, to change my direction.

To confess means actually "to agree with God as to His opinion of." In the old days when a race was run, many people in the grandstand would argue as to who was the real winner, for their angle of vision did not enable them to see the result clearly, so a judge was engaged to stand at the finish line and give the definite word as to the winner. This is the idea of which John speaks. To agree with God means to see our sins as God sees them, to look at them through His eyes. Pray that God will give you a holy hatred for sin. If you would see sin as God sees it, go not to the skid row, the brothel, or the alley, but go to Calvary and there see the cross from God's angle. See sin as God sees it, for there is the epitome of God's hatred for sin. Pray that God will help you to see Calvary through His eyes.

If you were to pick up your baby from a crib and find him cold in death with a rattlesnake coiled in one corner of the crib about to strike again, you would not take the snake to your breast and fondle it, you would destroy it. You would hate it with every fiber of your being for what it had done to your child. Ask God to help you see your sins and to hate them as He hates them because of what sin has done to His Son.

Why do we sin? Because we must? Because we

are forced into it? No! We sin because we enjoy it. The gossip enjoys his gossip. Many times we say, "Did you hear what happened to so and so? Oh, I was so sorry to hear it," when in reality we were not sorry at all. We enjoyed hearing it. Our own pride told us that we were better than so and so because it did not happen to us, and our gossiping tongue had something to talk about.

We lie because it serves a purpose. We are proud because we love ourselves. That is the way we look at our sins. But all this time God did not enjoy my lying, He did not like my jealousy, He did not find my pride desirable at all. God looked at my sins from a different angle than I did. To confess means to tell God that I did it, to get an agreement with Him, to look at my sin from His view and see that it was wrong, to change my mind about it, and to stop doing it. This is much more than telling God what He already knows.

It follows that if we have honestly done this, we have the assurance of His word that He accepts our repentance, our confession, and that our sins are forgiven. Do not doubt God. Take Him at His word. I may not always feel that I am an American, but still I am. Remember when you held your first-born in your arms and said, "It doesn't feel like he's really mine?" However he was yours—not because you felt like it or did not feel like it, but because the physical law of birth had taken place. Remember when you first married and said, "It doesn't seem real"? But it was real, not because of a feeling, but because a fact of law had taken place. So it is with the forgiveness of our sins. When they are confessed and genuinely forsaken, His forgiveness is not contingent upon our feelings but upon His word. God said it, I believe it, and that settles it.

There are two types of conviction for sin. Conviction is that troubled feeling that we have done wrong and need forgiveness. To convict means to make aware of, to be reminded of our sins. Before you have confessed your sins, but are reminded of them, this conviction is the plain pleading of the Holy Spirit of God. Dear Christian, do not try to hide from it. Do not try to pass it off as a little thing. To have blessed fellowship with God, one must please Him even in the smallest things. Our every thought, desire and act, must be brought into submission by the Holy Spirit. When you are reminded of the slightest wrong, forsake it, confess it, repent of it, kill it, despise it, destroy it, else the sore may become a cancer, the thought a personality, the deed a life. In these days when men compromise so with sin, legalize it, excuse it, philosophize about it, and in every way explain it away, we must constantly deal with our sins as realities that break fellowship between the believer and his God.

After you have genuinely confessed your sins, be assured that they are forgiven. You may not feel like it, but the feeling of assurance will grow. Be assured that while our feelings fluctuate, He has given His promise and His word changes not.

If after we have confessed our sins there still remains a conviction for them, one of two things is true. Either it was not a true confession (and we need to go back and examine our motives and make certain that our intent was right and that to the best of our ability by God's help we did confess, repent and forsake them) or the conviction is coming from somewhere else other than the Holy Spirit. In the latter case, it would be conviction from Satan. The Bible says that he is the accuser of the brethren and finds no little pleasure in the constant troubling of hearts over the memory of past sins. If you find this to be a problem, remember the words of James when he said, "Resist the devil, and he will flee from you" (James 4:7). Martin Luther was so troubled with the memory of sins which he knew to be forgiven that he flung a bottle of ink at the wall and his supposed picture of Satan. Just say, "Devil, you cannot deceive me. Satan, you are a liar. You cannot convict me, my sins are confessed and forgiven." And you will find him to be a coward. Quote I John 1:9 again. Make it your own in your heart. The devil cannot long resist the Word of the Lord. Ask in faith that God will fight this battle for you and ask Him to help you resist the devil.

If the memory and conviction of past sins you know to be forgiven persists, write down the sin or sins which trouble you on a piece of paper, go to the sink, light a match, and burn the paper. As the flame engulfs the paper, pray this in your heart, "Lord, just as definitely as this fire burns this piece of paper, do I claim the all-powerful cleansing blood of Christ Thy Son to burn my sins and cover them eternally." This visual aid will help your heart to know what your mind already believes.

There are three different kinds of sins that require three different types of confession. The first is personal sin. That is the sin no one knows about but you, and should only be confessed to the Lord. There is private sin that includes someone else but not the general public, and public sins in which many have been offended. If everyone knows about your sin, they will have been offended, and your

Christian testimony impaired. It is not enough to confess it to God, but it should be confessed publicly and public restitution made. If it is a private thing that only one or two know about, it is not enough to confess it to God, but it should be confessed and made right to the individuals concerned.

A good principle to follow in the confession of sins is this: Don't make the confession of the sin worse than it is but do make it as bad as it is. Make certain that restitution has been made to those who have been offended. Public confessions of personal sins are never wise and often do much harm.

When you take a black object and cover it with red cellophane, the sunshine through the paper will turn the blackness as white as snow. Just that definitely, when we receive Jesus and His cleansing blood for the atonement of our sins, the sunlight of God's all-seeing eye shining through the crimson blood of His Son, makes the blackness of our sins as white to Him as the new driven snow. Claim it, rejoice in it, live in it. "If we say that we have no sin, we deceive ourselves, and the truth is not in us" (I John 1:8). But "the blood of Jesus Christ his Son cleanseth us from all sin" (I John 1:7).

CHAPTER 9

ASKING

A famous book has pointed out that the only real praying is asking, and that confession of sin, praise, thanksgiving, are other than true prayer. I have no quarrel with this, it may or may not be correct.

We are not concerned with the technicality of names but with the reality of learning to pray. In the Lord's Prayer, we are taught to ask. Over and over our Lord beseeches us to ask. We are told to ask for our daily bread, our breath, health, and everyday things of life. David has said, "I have been young, and now am old; yet have I not seen the righteous forsaken, nor his seed begging bread" (Psalm 37:25). God takes care of His own. Though you never again ask for food, you will probably not starve to death. Though you never again ask for water nor thank Him for it, you will probably never die of thirst.

But while asking for the everyday sustenances is not primarily the means by which we receive them, it is the means by which we are brought to realize from whence cometh our blessings. The atheist down the street will probably live physically as well as you, perhaps a little better; but if you ask God for your daily bread, you will be more blessed than he. If my children never ask for a thing, they will receive all of their needs and more, but how much better will they be if they learn to appreciate the source of those gifts.

As in the confession of sin, two categories might be suggested. First is petition, the things we want for ourselves; the second, intercession, things we desire for other people.

Petition can be classified, once again, as both physical and spiritual. As you daily ask God for physical blessings, consider the difference between desire and need. Paul said, "My God shall supply all your need according to his riches in glory by Christ Jesus" (Philippians 4:19). You may be confident that if something is necessary for the carrying out of His will in your life, God is ready to give it. Would you hire a gardener and then not grant him the tools with which to do that which you expect of him? "And this is the confidence that we have in him, that, if we ask any thing according to his will, he heareth us" (I John 5:14). But He goes a step farther and declares through the psalmist, "Delight thyself also in the Lord; and he shall give thee the desires of thine heart" (Psalm 37:4). The fulfillment of these desires may be granted on this condition. If they are not mere whims to bring only momentary satisfaction or glory to us but are rather true desires to accomplish more good and live more fully to His glory, then it will be in accordance with His will. Only a careful searching of your heart can allow you to know the motivation that prompts your prayer.

Then there is intercession, asking for spiritual things for others. You can always be assured that you pray in faith in the will of God when you pray "Thy kingdom come. Thy will be done in earth" (Matthew 6:10). His will is for justice, charity, patience, and good for all, for He indeed is a good God. You can pray in faith when you pray for men to be reconciled with each other, for broken homes to be mended, for lives racked by disappointment and failure to be made at peace with God. You can pray for spiritual power and blessings upon loved ones, friends, and church in faith, and for the prosperity of the kingdom of God when you pray, "Thy will be done in earth."

Intercession, praying for others, is perhaps the greatest ministry in all the world. Only time will reveal what has been wrought by the prayers of the saints of God all over the world whose names have never been heralded before the public.

What would you say was the most common prayer offered in evangelical churches by lay people? Probably it is that the glorious light of the Gospel will shine on the unconverted and that they will be won for Christ. However, if you will again read carefully the pages of the New Testament you will find that the commands to pray for the unconverted are few and far between. The New Testament exhorts that prayer, supplication, giving of thanks and intercession be made for all men (I Timothy 2:1). The psalmist declared, "Ask of me, and I shall give thee the heathen for thine inheritance" (Psalm 2:8). Here are two definite commands to pray for the unsaved. Others will be more difficult to come by. The great apostle to the Gentiles said, "Brethren, my heart's desire and prayer to God for Israel is, that they might be saved" (Romans 10:1). But the word here interpreted prayer is more of a wish, a desire, a heartfelt longing, than a spoken prayer.

Now do not misunderstand. I do not mean to imply that we are not to pray for the unconverted. On the contrary, the salvation of the unbeliever will perhaps be the motivation behind most of our praying. But the general teaching of the New Testament is that we are to pray for ourselves in order that we become right, that we become channels through which God can work. When we pray, we do not convince God that He ought to convict men. He already desires this. The problem is that He has no one to work through. Prayer does not change God so much as it changes you.

As you pray, make your petitions known to God. Tell Him the one for whom you are praying and ask that He deal with his heart. But then, rather than repeat that petition over and over, quickly turn the spotlight of prayer on your own heart and spend most of your time letting God empty you, cleanse you, and fill you so that you might be the instrument through which that one is reached.

There are three factors to consider when praying for others—God, you, and the individual. If the person remains an unbeliever after you have prayed, does the trouble lie with God? Is it that He does not care, that He is powerless, to deal with that person? No, for He is all powerful and all compassionate. Is the trouble with the unsaved one? Is it that he is too hard? No, for the sweet river of the sunshine of God's love is able to melt the stoniest heart over which it flows. The difficulty then, obviously lies with us. When the Holy Spirit first came into my heart and did the work of regeneration, He took up His abode there permanently. However, rather than filling and overflowing me so I could be a blessing to others, much of the time He was crowded by sin into one corner of my heart. We are told, "Grieve not the holy Spirit," (Ephesians 4:30), and "Quench not the Spirit," (I Thessalonians 5:19). Sin, worldliness, faithlessness—all these things grieve Him and crowd Him into one corner of our heart, where He is quenched and unable to flow freely through us.

How does the Spirit of God move in a church service? How does He deal with the unreached? Is it through the song book, the organ, the pew, the pulpit, the lights? No, He uses us. God seldom uses things. He must have someone with whom to cooperate, someone through whom He can carry out His will, someone that will give himself up to be a conductor for the Spirit of grace. The Bible tells us, "From within him shall flow rivers of living water" (John 7:38 a.s.v.). What a promise! What potential! But in reality there is barely a trickle of power going through most of us and little outward fruit of the indwelling Spirit of God. We need not pray for others nearly as much as we need to pray for ourselves. A great preacher of another day said, "I have more trouble with myself than anyone else I know." The Apostle Paul said, "Oh wretched man that I am! who shall deliver me from the body of this death?" (Romans 7:24). Quickly he answers his question, "I thank God through Jesus Christ our Lord" (Romans 7:25). Ask God to form afresh the Lord Jesus in all His beauty and power in your innermost being, that you might pray His prayers, think His thoughts, desire what He desires. This is the secret of praying for others. Oh, that God would raise up men and women so able to cooperate with Him, so willing to be yielded, that He might perform His perfect will through them. The world has yet to see what God can do with one man completely yielded to Him.

After you have made your petition known to God and have done the work of the intercessor, you are still not finished with that which relates to asking. One final step remains—the affirmation or receiving in advance the assurance that our prayers will be answered. Have you really prayed in faith? Are you confident that your requests lie within the will of God? Then you need not hesitate to thank Him that He is going to answer. When you go to the bank to cash a check you do not hesitate to expect the funds. Why? Because you have confidence in the one who wrote the check and confidence in the bank's ability to cover it. You merely present your claims and expect the results. To receive in advance is to assure God of your faith and to build your own faith. Thanking God in advance is to affirm, strongly assert, and confirm our confidence in the forthcoming answer. Filling your heart with positive thoughts and positive faith will help to insure that God will bestow that same faith upon the individual for whom you are praying.

If you pray for a person who is ill, don't labor over thoughts and prayers of his sickness, but think and pray of the health that Christ gives. When you think of one with a broken arm, don't think of the break, but pray and thank God for the healing power of Calvary and the use to the glory of God that the healed arm can effect. This is positive praying.

In 1963 many mine disasters occurred around the world. Over and over again came the good news that a hole was being bored through the earth and a tube of air and supplies was being passed to the miners. This is the work of the intercessor—drilling a hole of positive faith by positive prayer through the barriers of doubt, troublesome thoughts and sin that shroud the one for whom we pray, that the sunshine of God's love may bear in upon him.

So when you have finished your prayer of intercession, do not get up, but rather stay on your knees and affirm over and over the answer to your prayer. Thank God in advance that He is going to answer and then get up and go your way, acting as though it had already happened. Do not check up on God or make other provision in case He doesn't do it. Merely believe Him, thank Him for the answer, receive it in faith and leave it with Him.

You need not hesitate to ask God if it's His will, for you will have already determined this before you have gone this far.

A review of chapter two will be helpful here.

CHAPTER 10

WAITING ON GOD

You can learn more about a friend from listening to him talk than by talking to him. We can learn much from God and about God through nature, through His Word, by the lives of those whom He has touched, and in many other ways. But nothing is as important as listening to the still, small voice that speaks to our hearts at the conclusion of our prayers. Perhaps you will find it more beneficial to wait upon the Lord at the beginning of your prayer than at the end. Personally, however, I find it more natural to wait upon the Lord at the close of my prayer time.

Prayer is a conversation, a union, an intermingling of two personalities. God speaks to me and I speak to Him. Suppose I were to call my wife long distance and say, "Hello, dear, how is the weather up there? Are the children all right? We are having a wonderful time here. I'll see you Sunday. I love you. Good-by." Have we had a conversation? Of course not, I have done all the talking. Many of us have never begun to know God because our prayer life has been one-sided. We have never learned to wait upon the Lord and let Him speak to us.

How many times have you sought the solution to some distressing situation by spasmodically turning through the pages of your Bible, trusting the Lord to lead you to the solution? You have probably found the words "wait upon God" and felt God was directing you to be patient and not get in a hurry for the solution to your problem. This, however, is not what is implied by waiting on God.

Waiting on God is not a mere abstract passing of time, it is a definite spiritual exercise during which, after having spoken to God, He, in turn, speaks to you. The Bible is filled with these directives: "Our soul waiteth for the Lord" (Psalm 33:20), "I will wait on thy name" (Psalm 52:9), "My soul waiteth upon God" (Psalm 62:1), "These wait all upon thee" (Psalm 104:27), "They that wait upon the Lord shall renew their strength" (Isaiah 40:31). Waiting upon God requires our entire being. It is not drifting into daydreaming, but is rather an exercise that demands our keenest attention, our most alert frame of mind and all of our soul's attention to the heavenly voice. I have never personally heard the voice of God, though I have heard some people, in whom I had the utmost confidence, say that they heard the audible voice of God speak to them. Perhaps they did, I do not know. God, however, speaks to me and will speak to most of us through thoughts, ideas, and impressions.

Can the conscientious person go by those inner feelings, that "something" that tells him, when no other directive is available, that he should or should not do a certain thing? Yes, on the condition that he is receptive to the touch of God's spirit with a heart that is made delicately sensitive by long periods of waiting before Him. This can only come by learning to wait upon the Lord. The Quakers call it "minding the checks." They mean that when a feeling comes that they should not do something, a spiritual check mark, it is best not to do it. This is the way God speaks to us.

I have asked many pastor friends to tell me in their own words why they accepted the call to the church they now serve. Without exception, they have replied that in the final analysis it was one thing. They just *felt* it was the thing to do. Something just *tells* us, makes us *feel* that we should or should not do certain things. Can the Christian go by this? Only on the condition that something within, be it heart, conscience, or whatever you choose to call it, has been kept responsive to the Lord by waiting. When we wait upon God, we do not wait *for* Him—He is already within. We wait *on* Him to be formed anew within us and for our desires, thoughts, and ambitions to be brought into submission to His.

How much suffering, how much disappointment we would save ourselves if we could learn the secret of waiting upon the Lord before we act.

Suppose for a moment that you earn $500 per month. You have a budget of $480 a month, leaving a balance of $20. You and your wife feel that she just must have the latest automatic washer that you have seen on sale, and it can be purchased for $19.95 per month. You can just make it. You rush down, make your purchase and for a while all is well. But suddenly you lose your job and the machine is lost. I believe that if you had waited upon the Lord about this and asked Him to guide you, when you went to look at the machine, somehow something would have said, "No, don't buy it." You would not have felt right about it and would have said to your mate, "I don't know why, but somehow I just don't feel right about buying it. Let's let it go." Then later on, when the job was lost, you would have understood why God guided you as He did and you should have been grateful for His infinite care and wise leadership. We could save ourselves much trouble if we would take God into account about our every decision. God is not just the God of the big things, but He longs to guide and be an ever-present help in each and every decision of life.

Unfortunately, there is not much that anyone can tell you about how to wait upon the Lord. You must learn by doing—by being quiet before Him, shutting out external thoughts and waiting for Him to impress your heart. However, perhaps it is just as well to learn how *not* to wait upon the Lord. There are some things not to do. There are pitfalls which Satan will lay before you as you attempt to wait upon God. If you can see what these are and what to do about them, then you can learn with the leadership of the Holy Spirit how to wait upon God. In waiting upon Him you will find at least four dangers.

The first difficulty you will probably encounter may seem a bit humorous at first but if you have prayed very long, you will have found it to be a problem. It is that of fatigue or drowsiness or just plain sleepiness. When your mind is actively engaged in prayer, the difficulty is not as great. However, when you attempt to empty your mind of your thoughts and desires and make your mind open to the voice of God, you will often have difficulty in staying awake. This may seem trivial, but is a very real problem for most people. (If you have not had difficulty in staying awake when you wait upon God, you have probably never prayed very much.) There is a very thin line between the state of mind that you are in when you wait upon God and the condition of mind when you take a little cat nap for a few minutes after dinner. Have you ever had the experience of lying down at one o'clock after a good noon meal for twenty or thirty minutes only to waken and find that it was three-thirty? By the same token, how many times have you begun to pray and prayed hour after hour, only to look at your watch and find that a mere ten minutes had passed? A person may wait before the Lord for an hour or two and never be conscious of the fact that he has been dozing and what seemed like connecting thoughts have actually come ten and twenty minutes apart.

In all sincerity I suggest that if you have difficulty in this manner, get up from your knees and go lay down and sleep for an hour, splash cold water on your face, drink something hot, take a brisk walk, or do some other tangible thing to remedy the problem. Then come back into the conscious presence of God at your very best. (Getting more sleep at night may help.) A Christian should not be up late Saturday night and then nod through church on Sunday morning. In all of our service, and most of all at prayer, we must conscientiously be alert and strive to give Him our best.

The second problem you will find, is that of a rambling mind or wandering thoughts due to psychological associations. Our minds are never empty. When they are not filled with conscious thoughts the subconscious mind takes over and we are thinking about something. Many times as you attempt to wait before the Lord, a thought will come to mind that has occurred before. This thought will suggest another and this, another, and this, still another, and you will find yourself completely afield from the task at hand. Or it may happen as your thoughts are filled with that which you desire. Suppose, for example, that you are waiting on the Lord for His leadership in the purchase of a home. You have been looking at many different houses and are not certain as to which one God would have you buy. As you wait upon the Lord for Him to impress you in this decision, naturally the picture of the house will appear on your mind. As you think about it, you see yourself driving up in front of that house in your automobile. This reminds you that in back of your car is your fishing gear and that you planned to go fishing last Saturday. This reminds you that it rained last Saturday and you are further reminded of a time when you were a little boy and went swimming in the rain, and on and on. What has happened? Rather than waiting on God about the house, you are off on a Saturday fishing trip or in the family swimming hole as a youngster. One thing has suggested another and your mind has wandered far from the original thought.

We can use psychological association to our advantage in memorizing facts and learning names, but Satan will use it to our disadvantage. When you encounter this difficulty, rather than keeping your mind centered upon the thing or things that at that moment might be concerning you, keep your mind centered upon something that has a religious connotation to you. Personally, I can imagine that I see a great white throne and God in all His majesty seated upon it, and myself kneeling before Him. Perhaps you will choose to picture in your mind's eye an open Bible, a cross, the steeple of a church, or some physical thing that has a spiritual connotation to you. If it is beneficial to you, if it is helpful when you pray, I am certain that God will be pleased.

When you go to God with a problem that has

many possible solutions, do not lay all of them before Him and ask which, but rather go to Him with each, one at a time. Suppose there are five homes you are considering. Don't picture all five at once and say, "Lord, which of these?" But rather, wait before Him with each. It is not difficult for God to select one out of the maze, but it is difficult for us to discern what He says. As you go to God with each, try to get your questions narrowed down to a simple yes or no answer. Ask Him about the first. If He says no, forget it. If He says yes, do it and forget the others. Make the solution as simple as this where possible.

When you have waited before the Lord and offered Him all the solutions that you can discern, and still do not feel His leadership, this does not mean that God has not heard your prayer. He may have an entirely different solution that you have never thought about. If you do not feel at peace about any of the five houses, ask God to guide you to another. This does not mean that another will pop into your mind if you have not sought it out, but it does mean that He will guide you if you will go seeking.

In E. Howard Cobb's book *Christ Praying*,[1] Mr. Cobb tells this wonderful story: "A little boy, about five years of age, enters his father's study. At once he asks, 'Daddy, I have lost my new book, will you ask Jesus to find it for me?'

"'Yes, I will,' replies his father, 'but you know that that does not mean that Jesus will bring it to you. You must let Him use your feet to take you to it, you must let Him use your eyes to see it, and your hands to pick it up; so if you do not find it the fault

[1] E. Howard Cobb, *Christ Praying* (London: Marshall, Morgan and Scott, Ltd., 1950).

will be yours, because you have not let Him use you.' A simple prayer is offered. The child hastens from the room. A few moments later a happy cry rings through the house, 'Daddy I've got it!' "

The third difficulty you will encounter is not so easily remedied. It is the problem of the subconscious mind. Psychologists tell us that ninety, ninety-five, even ninety-eight per cent of all that we have ever heard, read, seen, or thought is retained. It is lodged deep in the subconscious mind and can be called to memory under certain conditions. One such condition is sleep. That is what dreams are. The conscious mind goes out and the subconscious mind takes over. You cannot dream or bring anything out of your subconscious mind that you have not knowingly or unknowingly placed there before. Some hidden fear, hidden thought, secret desire or ambition may come out into the conscious mind. When you are waiting on the Lord, the mind is passive. Consequently, the devil will make a great use of the subconscious mind and recall to your memory many things which you had completely forgotten. The power of the subconscious mind is indeterminable. Today women give birth to children under hypnosis. Operations are performed under hypnosis. When the subconscious mind is affected, strange things may happen.

A young man is seated on an airplane or a bus and casually glances through a current magazine. He spends only a few seconds on each page, but there, almost unknown to him, will be inscribed on his subconscious mind the things he sees. There is a picture of a baseball stadium in New York, a church in South America, a politician in London, a bathing beauty in Hollywood, an oil well in Texas. He throws the magazine thoughtlessly aside and goes on to other things. That night he gets on his knees, begins to pray and wait upon the Lord. What do you think the devil is going to bring out of his subconscious mind? The South American church? The English politician? You know as well as I what the answer will be.

As you look in the mirror at the beginning of the day, a thought of pride flashes across your mind. As you drive to the grocery store in a moment of impatience, hatred flashes through your heart toward an irresponsible driver. Many unpleasant situations occur throughout the day. We pass them out of our mind and in a moment are unaware of their existence, but the devil is most aware of them and as we begin to pray, will very quickly begin to recall them to our conscious minds.

To this difficult problem there is a glorious solution for the child of God. As you begin to pray ask God to cleanse not only your heart and mind and soul, your tongue, and every part of your being, but also to cleanse even your *subconscious* mind in the blood of Jesus Christ. Ask Him by the power of the blood to subdue every evil thought and desire of which you are not conscious. You will find that the powers of evil that garrison themselves into militant activity when the child of God is upon his knees will flee in cowardice before the all-cleansing power of the blood of Christ!

The fourth pitfall you will encounter is that of evil spirits or stray spirits at work in the world. The Bible teaches that the devil and his emissaries are ever at work to destroy the effectual service of the child of God. Sometimes thoughts and ideas will come, impressions will burn upon our mind, and we will wonder whether they are actually *from the Holy Spirit* or *from the devil*. Do not think that the devil is a myth. He is called Satan, Lucifer, Beelzebub, the prince of the air, a roaring lion, a sower of tears, a wolf. He lies, he talks, he thinks, he acts, he quotes Scriptures, he was resisted by Job, Jesus, and the disciples. He is as real as God the Father, Jesus the Son, and the Holy Spirit. He hates you and God and dains to thwart the purpose of God at every possible corner. Do not think that he is, as pictured in medieval mythology, a little man with a red suit, horns, a tail, and a pitchfork. The Bible tells us that he comes transformed as an angel of light (II Corinthians 11:14). The very word Lucifer means, "light bearer," or "one who shines." While he is a beautiful and attractive light, he is a deceptive light. We might have occasion to question whether the impression we have is of God or of the devil, for indeed he can lead us astray and give us desires, under the guise of light, and we may never know whether they are of God or not.

Wouldn't it be wonderful if, at the time of prayer, we were able to enter into a concrete vault or a steel room through which the devil could not penetrate? Ah, but though this is impossible, there is one shield through which he cannot penetrate. Ours is a spiritual warfare against spiritual wickedness in which we employ spiritual armor. Ephesians 6:10-17, tells us of our warfare and our armor against the devil:

> Finally, my brethren, be strong in the Lord, and in the power of his might.
> Put on the whole armour of God, that ye may be able to stand against the wiles of the devil.
> For we wrestle not against flesh and blood,

but against principalities, against powers, against the rulers of the darkness of this world, against spiritual wickedness in high places.

Wherefore take unto you the whole armour of God, that ye may be able to withstand in the evil day, and having done all, to stand.

Stand therefore, having your loins girt about with truth, and having on the breastplate of righteousness;

And your feet shod with the preparation of the gospel of peace;

Above all, taking the shield of faith, wherewith ye shall be able to quench all the fiery darts of the wicked.

And take the helmet of salvation, and the sword of the Spirit, which is the word of God.

So there is one barrier through which evil spirits and stray thoughts cannot penetrate and that is the shield of faith, whereby we quench all of the attacks of the wicked one. As you begin to wait upon God, ask God in faith, believing, to put about your mind the shield of faith through which the devil cannot penetrate. Tell Him that you believe that He will protect you with the shield of faith by your faith in His word and the power of the Spirit, that you are going to act upon every impression as though it came from Him, and that you are trusting Him to allow only those thoughts to come which are His thoughts. Then, if you have sincerely offered yourself to Him, you can go your way, act upon the thoughts you have, and be assured that you are doing the will of God. The words, "Above all, taking the shield of faith," do not mean, "most important of all," but rather "over all" or "around all."

After you have prayed and waited before the Lord

other things will come into your mind and you will again want to speak to your Heavenly Father. Do not fear that He will be impatient because you come often, for He has no greater desire than to hear the prayers of His children. Prayer, then, will indeed become a conversation, a union of two, and a blending into one of separate desires and thoughts. When you know God and His will you can with the utmost of confidence, with no uncertainty, approach boldly the throne of grace and pray with the positive faith that brings the result for which you so earnestly long.

Chapter 11

IN JESUS' NAME

As Christians, we believe that the prayers that God answers are those that are prayed through the Lord Jesus. Man can only get in touch with God through the media of the God-man, Jesus the Nazarene.

We have all attended sporting events and civic engagements and heard someone finish his prayer thusly, "And Dear Lord, bless us this day, Amen." Nothing leaves me flatter. I like to hear a man pray—God implores that we pray—in the name of Jesus Christ.

I know that one will say "But all that I do is in His name and I feel in my heart that I pray in His name." Yes, but while it is more than those three words "in Jesus' name" tacked on the end of a prayer, rather what they mean, still they are to be in your prayer.

To pray in Jesus' name, means simply to pray in, by, with the help of, through, Jesus. It is to desire what He desires, to pray His prayer. The Bible promises much in the name of Jesus. It tells us "There is none other name under heaven given among men, whereby we must be saved" (Acts 4:12). And again, "Whosoever shall call upon the name of the Lord shall be saved" (Romans 10:13).

Why is so much promised through the name of Jesus Christ? What is a name? A name is the person it represents. For example, if someone says the name "Barbara," I have no reaction or if they speak the name "Hazel," still there is nothing. But when someone says "Uldine," immediately there is the image, the love, and all the personality of my wife. That is the name of the one I love. "Uldine" is no different from any other name, but what the name implies to me is different. When someone says "Billy, The Kid," I see an image of a western villain, but when they say "Billy Graham," I think of a great evangelist. The name implies the individual. The suggestion of one name can literally cause physical reaction in your body, produced by hatred, jealousy, or love. Would you name your child "Jezebel?" Of course not. Jezebel is just as good a name as Judy or Jo Ann, but the implications are not the same.

I have tried to witness to people who were using profanity. I have spoken to them of the church, of religion, of conversion, of sin, judgment, and the cross. But when I use the name "Jesus" I have found that their profanity stopped and an entirely different atmosphere is established. To pray in Jesus' name then is simply to pray in the Lord Jesus.

Were I to go to the First National Bank of New York City and write a note saying "I would like to borrow a million dollars" and sign my name, "John R. Bisagno," the teller would look at the note and laugh and push it back through the window. You see my name is not worth a million dollars there or anywhere else, for I am not worth a million dollars. But let me write the same note and then at the bottom of the page another person writes "O.K. by me" and signs "John D. Rockefeller." Now I will get the money because I am not coming in my merit, my worth, my name, but I come upon the basis of the merit of one that is worth a million dollars.

What if I do not want this money for myself? I want it for Mr. Rockefeller. He is my friend. I plan to spend all of this money on him. It is for his sake, not mine that I make my request. I still won't get the money, because it cannot be for his sake but must be in his name. I realize that to most of us the meaning is the same, but we are not promised answered prayer "for Jesus' sake" but "in Jesus' name." Of course, everything we do should be for the glory of God and for the sake of His dear Son, Jesus. Yet the Bible qualifications for answered prayer are "in Jesus' Name." Privately and publicly, never be ashamed of your testimony to the name of Jesus Christ. Think what it means. Feel what it means. Imply it? Yes; but say it audibly for your good and for the benefit of those about you. "Whatsoever ye shall ask in my name, that will I do, that the Father may be glorified in the Son" (John 14:13).

CHAPTER 12

A FINAL WORD

Early in my ministry God placed upon my heart a burden for prayer. Since that time I have been further impressed, by books and the lives of great Christians, that positive prayer is the power that never fails. This book consequently was designed to be brief. I do not want you to spend so much time reading *how* to pray that you have no time to pray. In bygone days, when revival fires burned across country after country, the one characteristic of the men and women that God used most was that of prayer. Some were not eloquent, were even slow of speech. Many were anything but educated, some even approached illiteracy. But they had one thing in common—they prayed. They didn't talk about praying (they were too busy praying to talk about it). They didn't write books about prayer or have prayer conferences, they prayed. I really do not feel that most of us need to know much more about praying. The difficulty is not in lack of knowledge, but is that we just do not pray. We do not need more information nearly as much as we need inspiration.

Jonathan Edwards preached and men cried and clung to the columns of the church for fear they would slide into an eternity without God. This man was not a great preacher. He wore thick glasses, read most of his sermons, and had awkward gestures. What most of us do not know is that he often spent ten, twelve, sometimes fifteen and eighteen hours on his knees in prayer before he preached.

Edward Payson prayed until grooves were worn in the floor by his knees. Luther rose before 4:00 A.M. to pray. David Brainerd, the great missionary to the Indians, would prostrate himself in the snow and pray until the snow melted beneath him. Oh, that God might raise up men and women like this today!

If you cannot give, you can pray. If you cannot see, you can pray. If you cannot hear, you can pray. If you cannot sing, you can pray. If you cannot preach, you can pray. There are no circumstances in which you will ever find yourself, no condition into which God will lead you but that victory cannot be found through prayer.

Allow me to share with you something very personal and precious to my heart. Before I entered the preaching ministry, I served the Lord for years in the field of religious music. Though I was far from home, without physical resources or visible hope for the future, when God called me to preach I responded immediately and was willing to trust Him in complete faith.

One evening in an upstairs room of the Belgravia Hotel in Belfast, Ireland, only two days before all physical resources would be gone, a telephone call came inviting me to conduct evangelistic services. These would begin on the following Sunday at the Immanuel Baptist Church. This was Tuesday. I accepted and began to prepare. When, on Friday, I called to check on the functioning of the committees and the distribution of the advertising for the meetings, I was informed that nothing had been done and that the people would not be told until Sunday morning that I was to come on Sunday night. I was disappointed, frightened, and desperately feared for the results. Realizing that only God could give a victory, I asked the pastor to call his people together at 8:00 Saturday night for a prayer meeting. Sixty-five of us met in a small room and began to pray. And oh, how they prayed. One by one, hour after hour, until the early hours of the morning, they earnestly besought God for His presence and power upon the services. With my heart greatly lifted in faith, I returned to my hotel room to rest through the day. That evening at 7:30, following a brief meeting with the pastor; we prepared to walk into the church sanctuary to begin the service. Suddenly, the pastor paused, put his arm about my shoulder, and with a look of fatherly sympathy, said, "Now, son. I don't want you to be discouraged, but my people don't like Yankee preachers over here. Furthermore, they have never seen an American invitation. They will not come forward as you may ask them to do. One other thing," he added, "I have not had a convert under my ministry in more than a year and you should not expect any tonight." Then as my heart sank, he added, "And there is just one more thing, this church has never been full in the twenty-seven years I have been here, and it won't be full for you, so don't expect much."

I tried to smile and said, "Thanks." It seemed that I could never get the courage to walk through that door and I said, "Dear Pastor, let us pause and pray just one more time." He prayed and then I prayed, more earnestly than I ever had, "Oh God," I said, "*If* I have made a mistake in following Thee, show me tonight. Let what this man says come true.

But" I added, "If Thou really art God, if You still answer prayer, if I can believe and trust Thee completely in faith for everything and in every way, then I want You to show me the greatest miracle I have ever seen," and we started through the door.

To my great joy I could not even reach the pulpit for the people. They were standing on the platform, around the choir, around the steps, in the aisles, everywhere. The church, that would hardly hold 250, was jammed with 400. I preached for about ten minutes and stopped. Then I said, "If anyone here tonight is willing to receive Christ as his Lord, in faith, right this moment, I want you to come down for prayer," and immediately thirteen people stood to their feet and pushed their way forward. There was no singing, no choir, no music at all. I stopped and said, "That's all, you are dismissed."

After dealing with the seekers, I went downtown to tell the story of my conversion to about 1200 at a city-wide, after-church, youth rally. Many others made decisions for Christ that night. I went home saying, "Thank You, Lord, it was a wonderful beginning, but I still don't believe it. Now Lord" I prayed, "they don't go to church in Ireland on Monday night. I want to see it again. If You are really a God that answers prayer, do it again tonight."

On Monday night the crowd was larger and fourteen came to the Lord. So mighty were the blessings of God that we extended the meetings to two, three, four, and finally five weeks. In the closing days we had to conduct two services a night to accommodate the crowds. People often stood on the steps of the church and listened through open doors and strained to hear through windows.

During the day we would sing and play in many

of Belfast's shipbuilding yards in open-air gospel services and often times crowds of five and ten grew to five hundred and eight hundred in twenty minutes, so mighty was the power and presence of God.

One night in the services a man from Wales who could barely understand a word I said asked his sister throughout the message, "What did he say?" "What was that?" "What is he saying?" She disgustedly replied, "Oh, be quiet, he's saying something about, if you want to receive Christ, come forward." Right in the middle of the service he stood and blurted out, "Oh, yes, I do," and began to run down the aisle. Before another word was spoken I said, "Let us stand and sing" and with only one verse, twenty-one grown men and women in that tiny church walked the aisle after him.

People left their jobs early, merchants closed their stores, and folks literally stood on the street corners and over backyard fences, talking, not about the preacher, not about the revival, but about the Lord. It is said that truck drivers and trolley operators would pass by the area of the church and begin to weep with conviction just being near the place where God was moving so mightily. After the meetings ended, I prepared to board the boat to sail to Scotland and a curtain flung open beside the dock, as over two hundred converts from that revival began to sing "God Be With You Till We Meet Again." Needless to say, that was the greatest thrill of my life. God *has* been with me and with them, and He is with you and will be with you in a way you have never known if you, as these people did, can learn the secret of the power of positive prayer.

Don't just read this book and set it aside, go to your knees and try what it says. It really works. First, repent of every sin in your life, then turn by faith to Jesus and receive God's dear Son as your own personal Saviour. Set out to discern His will and when you know it, believe and receive in faith from Him the answer to your prayer and you can know a life with joys that are beyond description. What potential is at the fingertips of every believer. As believers, we are one with Christ. By union with Him the life we now live in the flesh we literally do live by the faith of the Son of God.

In Russia many years ago an elderly mother was being moved from her home into the poor home provided by the state. One of the men assisting in moving the furniture noticed on a piano a picture of a young man. "Why, isn't this your son, John?" he asked.

"Yes," said the mother, "he's gone to America and I am left alone."

"But I happen to know that he has done very well," replied the man. "Hasn't he ever written you? Didn't he send you means? Has he not taken care of you better than this?"

"Oh, he's written," she said, "but all he ever sent were little pictures. I suppose they are only pictures of his friends, but they do look rather old for John."

"You haven't thrown them away, have you?" he said.

"Oh, no," she replied, "I've saved every one waiting for my boy to come home and tell me who they were, but I guess he isn't coming."

Together they walked into the bedroom and there on the poor woman's wall were hundreds and thousands of five, ten and twenty dollar bills. She was rich, but she was a rich fool.

Potentially, all of the grace, attributes, virtues,

and powers of God the Father, and of Christ His Son are ours. Do not ask God to give you more faith. You do not need more faith. You need to learn to appropriate the faith you already have. Receive Him, know Him, find His will, ask Him to do it, thank Him for having done it, and go your way, rejoicing that the victory is already won, the answer already given. My prayer for you is that you might, by learning to practice the principles set forth in this little book, know the power that is your birthright, the power of positive praying.